For the child in all of us

In loving memory of Dominique Corbasson

(1958–2018)

Little Audrey's Daydream
The Life of Audrey Hepburn

Written by

Sean & Karin Hepburn Ferrer

Illustrated by

Dominique Corbasson & François Avril

PRINCETON ARCHITECTURAL PRESS · NEW YORK

I was born on May 4, 1929, in Brussels, Belgium,
a charming town famous for its chocolates, cookies, and cartoons—
heaven. Two funny-looking people were smiling down at me.

Within a few days of my birth, I awoke
with a terrible cough—adults called it "whooping cough."
It got worse and worse until I stopped breathing
and started to turn blue. My mother desperately started
slapping me on the bottom. I let out a loud cry
and started to breathe again.

This became my favorite story.

I often asked my mother to tell me about the time
when I stopped breathing and turned blue. I especially loved
the part about the spanking having saved my life.
Spanking is really bad. But in this case, it was really good.

My family soon moved to Holland.
Holland is a small country next to Belgium, famous for its windmills.
Today it's called the Netherlands. In the winters everything froze,
and I loved skating on the rivers to get to school.
Skating is like dancing, and it was my dream to become a ballerina.

One day a huge war broke out and soldiers
invaded Holland. Their leader was a horrible little man
with a tiny mustache who screamed all the time.

Living in a country at war means there are soldiers
everywhere who ask you who you are, what you
are doing, and where you are going. Grown-ups called it
"the Occupation." I saw fear in their eyes.

Every night planes flew over and dropped bombs.
So we hid in our cellars, which most families turned into
living rooms with sofas and radios. A little dust would fall from
the ceiling every time a bomb exploded close to home.

Sometimes friends of the family would let me ride
their bicycle to take little notes across town.
These notes were so secret that I had to hide them in my shoes.
I thought they must have been secret love letters.
It turned out they were notes for our allies and the Resistance.

I was able to dance in theaters, sometimes for
large audiences. When the performances were finished
nobody clapped their hands. It wasn't because they
didn't like it—they simply didn't want to attract the attention
of the enemy soldiers. So they just smiled in the dark.

There was little to eat because the soldiers
took all our food. So we ate green-pea bread,
dog cookies, and tulip bulbs.
Holland is famous for its beautiful tulips.

Now I spend a lot of time in bed since there is little food and no fuel for heat. My parents say that it helps "preserve our calories." Sometimes I read in bed for hours.

I miss my life before the war.
I miss playing outside with my friends and skating
to school. So I lie in bed and daydream.

On this particular day I begin to dream about
my life once the war is over…

I find the best ballet school so that I can become
a prima ballerina. I am the best dancer in the class…
although I know it isn't very polite to be
the center of attention.

I dance, sing, and act. I run up to the attic,
dig through that ancient trunk filled with elegant clothes
and hats, dress up, and perform.

I perform in little plays and musicals,
and soon I am discovered and given a part in a film.
I love the few films I saw before the war.
The movie palace is a wonderful place to smile in the dark.

I play a princess who escapes from her castle,
a poor flower girl who becomes a lady, a librarian—I so love books—
who becomes a fashion model, and a regular country girl
who moves to a big city and becomes quite a stylish dresser.
I finally get to sing *and* dance.

Now I am famous. Famous means everyone knows you, or thinks they do, and likes you a lot.

When I grow up, I decide to have a family of my own.
I love babies. I always try to pick them up out of their prams
to hug them. My mother scolds me when I do.

I want my family to live in a country where
there will never be wars.

I have seen postcards of Switzerland and like
it because it is a neutral country. A neutral country
is one where war is not allowed. Switzerland
has beautiful mountains, cows for milk and chocolate,
and clean air, so I decide to live there. My children
and I take long walks in the mountains, and
no one asks us who we are, what we are doing,
or where we are going.

My children come with me on movie sets, and my life is perfect.
When they are old enough to go to school—I so miss going to school—
I decide to stop making films in order to stay home and just be a "Mum."

I become a full-time Mum, taking my
boys to school and shopping for books and socks.
Boys always need more socks.

My boys continue to grow and soon go off into the world.

I have a good life and a happy family,
and I consider going back to making films.
But what about the other children who might
still be a little bit sad and lonely?
I want to help a child smile in the dark.

I travel to countries that are still at war,
and I help to feed hungry children.
I come home to tell everyone how truly awful war is.
I do this work with all my heart because I know what
it's like to be hungry. Being a movie star was fun,
but caring for children is much nicer.

I feel good about this chapter in my life,
and my boys are proud of me.

My daydream ends when I hear my Mum calling out,
"It's bedtime." I turn off the light and smile in the dark as I think
about what it means to be loved for being a good person.

And with that final thought, I fall asleep.

MORE ABOUT AUDREY HEPBURN

Audrey Hepburn (May 4, 1929–January 20, 1993) was a British actress and humanitarian. She was born in Brussels, Belgium, and grew up in the Netherlands during the Second World War. During that time she suffered from hunger and malnutrition.

She rose to stardom in the romantic comedy *Roman Holiday* (1953), for which she was the first actress to win an Oscar, a Golden Globe Award, and a BAFTA (British Academy of Film and Television Arts) Award for a single performance. She was twenty-three. Throughout her career, she won three BAFTA Awards for Best British Actress in a Leading Role. In recognition of her film career, she received BAFTA's Lifetime Achievement Award, the Golden Globe Cecil B. DeMille Award, the Screen Actors Guild Life Achievement Award, and the Special Tony Award. She remains one of only fifteen people to have ever won an Emmy, Grammy, Oscar, and Tony Award (EGOT). Recognized as a film and fashion icon, she was ranked by the American Film Institute as the third-greatest female screen legend of the past one hundred years.

Later in life she devoted much of her time to UNICEF, to which she had contributed since 1954. She worked in some of the poorest communities of Africa, South America, and Asia between 1988 and 1992. In December 1992, she received the US Presidential Medal of Freedom in recognition of her work as a UNICEF Goodwill Ambassador. A month later, she died of appendiceal cancer (PMP) at her home in Switzerland at the age of sixty-three. She is one of thirty-nine individuals to have been awarded the Jean Hersholt Humanitarian Oscar for "outstanding contributions to humanitarian causes."

The Story Behind the Daydream

After having written the *New York Times* best seller *Audrey Hepburn, An Elegant Spirit*, her son Sean Hepburn Ferrer wanted to take her story into the realm of fables.

Having been graced with three perfect acts—first a Cinderella-like youth and discovery, then a career as one of the world's best-loved film legends and style icons, and finally her third act as a humanitarian and a UNICEF ambassador, a confirmation of her inner grace and compassion—her life naturally offered the perfect spine for a modern-day fairy-tale.

Ferrer, together with his wife, Karin, with whom he not only shares his life but also his day-to-day business activities, distilled Hepburn's rich life into this essential story.

Hepburn was born in Brussels, the global center of the illustration and cartoon world, and it made sense to have two legends like Dominique Corbasson and her husband, François Avril, illustrate her story.

This was Corbasson's final work as she was sick with terminal cancer. She worked to complete *Little Audrey's Daydream* until a few days before passing.

Dominique Corbasson and François Avril

Dominique Corbasson was an artist and illustrator who worked as a designer for Habitat, the Galeries Lafayette, Chanel, Hermès, Tiffany & Co., and many other global brands before deciding to devote her time to children's and illustrated books.

Today, her work is still widely exhibited in art galleries from Paris to Tokyo.

Her delicate line, whether in paint or colored crayon, is light, flowing, instinctive, and decidedly modern. Her townscapes and landscapes, often highly detailed, are buzzing with the life she captures so well, whether on a hot summer day or a snowy winter afternoon.

Dominique Corbasson bathes in the atmosphere, drawing nourishment and observing with the total and sincere attention that makes her work so special. Her unique sketches of Parisians and her visions of California, New York, London, Tokyo, and even Scotland are the vibrant testimonials of her unique talent and signature.

François Avril was born in 1961 in Paris. A graduate of École Nationale Supérieure des Arts Appliqués et des Métiers d'Art, he has produced children's books, comics, and many limited-edition prints. He regularly exhibits his work on canvas or on paper in Paris, Geneva, Amsterdam, Brussels, Dinard, Strasbourg, and Tokyo.

PUBLISHED BY
Princeton Architectural Press
202 Warren Street, Hudson, New York 12534
www.papress.com

ISBN 978-1-61689-991-2

Design: Jack Durieux

FOR PRINCETON ARCHITECTURAL PRESS
Editors: Amy Novesky and Kristen Hewitt
Design coordination: Paul Wagner

Library of Congress Cataloging-in-Publication Data
available upon request.